DISCOVER
BUGS

Titles in the *Discover Animals* series:

Discover Big Cats
ISBN-13: 978-0-7660-3473-0
ISBN-10:   0-7660-3473-9

Discover Bugs
ISBN-13: 978-0-7660-3472-3
ISBN-10:   0-7660-3472-0

Discover Sharks
ISBN-13: 978-0-7660-3474-7
ISBN-10:   0-7660-3474-7

Discover Snakes
ISBN-13: 978-0-7660-3471-6
ISBN-10:   0-7660-3471-2

DISCOVER ANIMALS

DISCOVER
BUGS

Monalisa Sengupta

Enslow Publishers, Inc.
40 Industrial Road
Box 398
Berkeley Heights, NJ 07922
USA
http://www.enslow.com

This edition published in 2009 by Enslow Publishers, Inc.

Original copyright © 2005 Really Useful Map Company (HK) Ltd.

Library of Congress Cataloging-in-Publication Data

Sengupta, Monalisa.
Discover bugs / Monalisa Sengupta.
p. cm. — (Discover animals)
Includes bibliographical references and index.
Summary: "Learn about a variety of helpful and harmful bugs and what
makes a bug an insect"—Provided by publisher.
ISBN 978-0-7660-3472-3
1. Insects—Juvenile literature. I. Title.
QL467.2.S46 2009
595.7—dc22
2008013865

Printed in China

10 9 8 7 6 5 4 3 2 1

To Our Readers: We have done our best to make sure all Internet Addresses in this book were active and appropriate when we went to press. However, the author and the publisher have no control over and assume no liability for the material available on those Internet sites or on other Web sites they may link to. Any comments or suggestions can be sent by e-mail to comments@enslow.com or to the address on the back cover.

Enslow Publishers, Inc., is committed to printing our books on recycled paper. The paper in every book contains 10% to 30% post-consumer waste (PCW). The cover board on the outside of each book contains 100% PCW. Our goal is to do our part to help young people and the environment too!

Photo and Illustration Credits: Q2AMedia

Cover Photos and Illustrations: Q2AMedia

Contents

Bug World

Bugs are creepy, crawly creatures that live in the garden, under stones, and even in your house. Officially called insects, bugs are small, six-legged animals with certain traits in common. There are over a million species or types of insects – much more than all the animal and plant types together! Some insects are considered "true bugs," which will be described later in the book.

■ The wings of the peacock butterfly are reddish-brown on top and dark brown to black underneath. They have special marks on the wings, which look like false eyes.

■ A dragonfly has four large wings that look like fine gauze. As it flies through the air, it holds its legs together to form a basket in which other insects are caught. The dragonfly can eat while flying.

Living zones

Look around anywhere and you are sure to find a bug. Insects can live almost anywhere on Earth – from hot tropical jungles to snow-capped mountains and scorching deserts. They can be found in caves and burrows deep in the ground, or flying high in the sky. Some insects can even live on an animal's body, or inside it!

Tasty bite

Most insects feed on plants. But they are usually not fussy about food and can eat almost anything. They are known to feed on fabrics, plaster, cork, face powder, other living things, and even toothpaste!

Secret of success

Bugs appeared on Earth long before humans. The secret of their ability to survive in just about any conditions lies in their small size, tough outer skeleton and adaptability. Bugs are not choosy about the places they live in or the things they eat. Bugs also have short lives. They quickly become adults and give birth to a large number of babies – each of them usually better survivors than their parents.

■ The black or black-and-orange burying beetles look out for dead mice and other small animals. They bury these animals so they can feed on them.

INTERESTING FACT!

Most insects are less than 0.24 inches (6 mm) long. The smallest ones include hairy-winged dwarf beetles. They can easily crawl through the eye of a needle, and are barely visible to the human eye!

Bugging us

We are constantly at war with insects. They annoy us, bite us, infect us with diseases, eat our food, and damage our property. But not all insects are harmful. A lot of them are of great value to us. Some help in pollination, while others serve as food for fish, birds and many other animals. In fact, life on Earth might not exist if all the insects were to disappear!

■ Despite their names, velvet ants are actually a species of wasp. The female velvet ant does not have any wings.

Inside Story

Although they come in various shapes, sizes and colors, all insects have a common body structure. Their body is divided into three main parts – head, thorax and abdomen. Insects have six legs, arranged in three pairs. They also have a pair of antennae and a tough, shell-like outer covering. Some insects even have wings.

■ Like with all other insects, the exoskeleton of a cockroach does not grow as it gets older. Hence, the exoskeleton becomes too tight and needs to be shed. The bug forms a new suit of armor underneath before it crawls out of the old suit.

A Madagascar hissing cockroach

Abdomen

A bug's abdomen contains its organs, which are very different from a human being's. Air enters the insect through a few pores in the exoskeleton. These pores are called spiracles. Oxygen is distributed to all areas of the body through breathing tubes. In humans, blood flows through special tubes called blood vessels. In bugs, though, blood flows throughout the body cavity.

Armor suit

Bugs have a shell-like outer covering over their soft bodies. This outer covering is called the exoskeleton. It is usually light and strong, and serves as a suit of armor that protects the bug. The muscles of the bug are attached to the inside wall of the exoskeleton.

INTERESTING FACT!

When insects walk, they usually move the middle leg on one side with the front and hind legs on the opposite side. In this way, they are always firmly supported – like a three-legged stool.

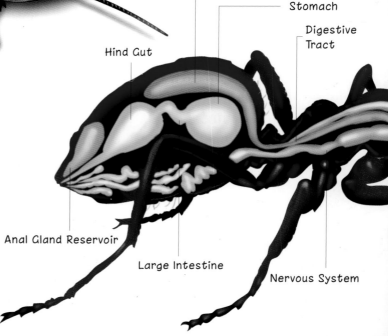

Social Stomach

Stomach

Digestive Tract

Hind Gut

Anal Gland Reservoir

Large Intestine

Nervous System

FACT FILE

Fastest-flying insect
Dragonfly; 60 mph (95 km/h)
Longest flight
Butterflies and locusts can fly
continuously for well over
100 miles (160 km). Tiny
fruit flies can fly for more
than five hours
Shortest flight
Honeybees can fly for only 15
minutes at a time
Wing speed
Large-winged butterflies
beat their wings 4 to 20 times
per second; houseflies, about
200 times; and some midges
about 1,000 times
per second
Fastest-moving insect
Cockroach; 3.35 mph
(5.40 km/h)

■ Insects that chew have powerful grinding jaws called mandibles. The jaws work sideways, not up and down as in humans. The jaws are also modified for sucking.

Heady matter

Most adult insects have two enlarged eyes, with a pair of antennae between them. They use these antennae to smell, taste and even hear. The head of a "true bug" includes mouthparts as well. These include special structures for feeding, which allow the bug to chew or suck.

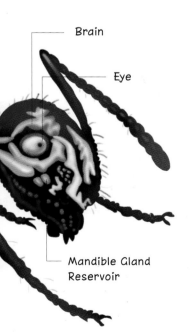

Brain

Eye

Mandible Gland
Reservoir

■ Bugs have compound eyes. While humans have just one lens, insects can have thousands of separate lenses. These combine to form a complete picture of what an insect sees.

Thorax

The thorax is the middle section of a bug's body. It supports the three pairs of legs and the wings, if present. Bugs can use their legs for running, grasping, digging or swimming.

Changing Times

Nearly every insect starts life as an egg. After hatching, the insect begins to grow and develops into an adult. During this process, most insects go through a series of amazing changes in form. The entire cycle – from egg to adult – takes only a few days for some species, and as long as 17 years for others.

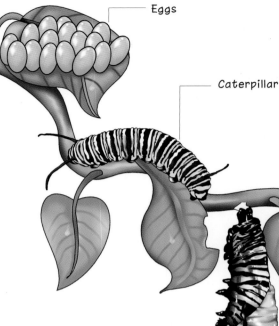

Eggs

Caterpillar

Caterpillar entering pupal stage

Growing up

After an egg hatches, it follows one of three patterns of growth and development, depending on its type. The simplest cycle occurs in a few kinds like silverfish and springtails. When the eggs of these insects hatch, the young ones look exactly like their parents, only smaller. These are called nymphs.

■ This is a trilobite larva, a female bug that grows to maturity while retaining juvenile or larval form.

Changing form

Other insects have a far different pattern of growth and development. The young look different from their parents and are called larvae. They change in form as they develop into adults. This change is called metamorphosis.

■ Cicadas plant their eggs in tree branches. On hatching, the nymphs fall to the ground and scurry into the soil, settling near the tree roots. They feed on the sap for 7 years. As they grow larger they molt their exoskeleton - revealing a newly formed one under it.

Types of metamorphosis

There are two kinds of metamorphosis. In incomplete metamorphosis, the nymphal stages look like the adult except that they don't have wings. The nymphs may also be a different color than the adults. In complete metamorphosis, on the other hand, young bugs do not look at all like the adults. The nymphs often live in different habitats, and feed on different things.

FACT FILE

Largest insect egg
0.5 inches (1.3 cm) - from the Malaysian stick insect
Average number of eggs
100 to 200 eggs during a lifetime
Largest layer of eggs
Termite; can lay 10,000 to 30,000 in a day
Smallest eggs
Tachinidae fly; length is less than 0.001 to 0.01 inches (0.002 to 0.02 cm)

Adult butterfly

Adult butterfly coming out of pupa

Pupa about to open

■ After a larva completes its growth, it stops eating and spins a cocoon – a protective covering – around its body. It then becomes a pupa. Inside the covering, it is broken down and re-formed into adult organs. After the change is complete, the pupal covering cracks open and the adult flies out.

Eggs of all shapes

Insect eggs have a variety of shapes and color patterns, but most are oval or round and are pale- or cream-colored. Insects lay their eggs singly or in batches. They usually lay them on or near food, which the young eat after they hatch.

INTERESTING FACT!

A pair of houseflies could produce millions of babies, if all of them lived! Attacks by parasites, predators, lack of food supply, and other factors prevent many of them from surviving.

■ The cockroach's egg case is the size and shape of a baked bean. It can contain from 10 to 20 eggs.

Insect – Or Not?

Not all small animals that crawl are insects. A spider is not an insect, and neither is a centipede. In fact, only those crawling creatures that have six legs and a body divided into three parts are called insects.

Caught in a web

Spiders are arachnids, and differ from insects in many ways. While spiders have eight legs, insects have six. A spider's body is divided into only two main parts, whereas an insect has three parts. Most insects have wings and antennae, but spiders do not.

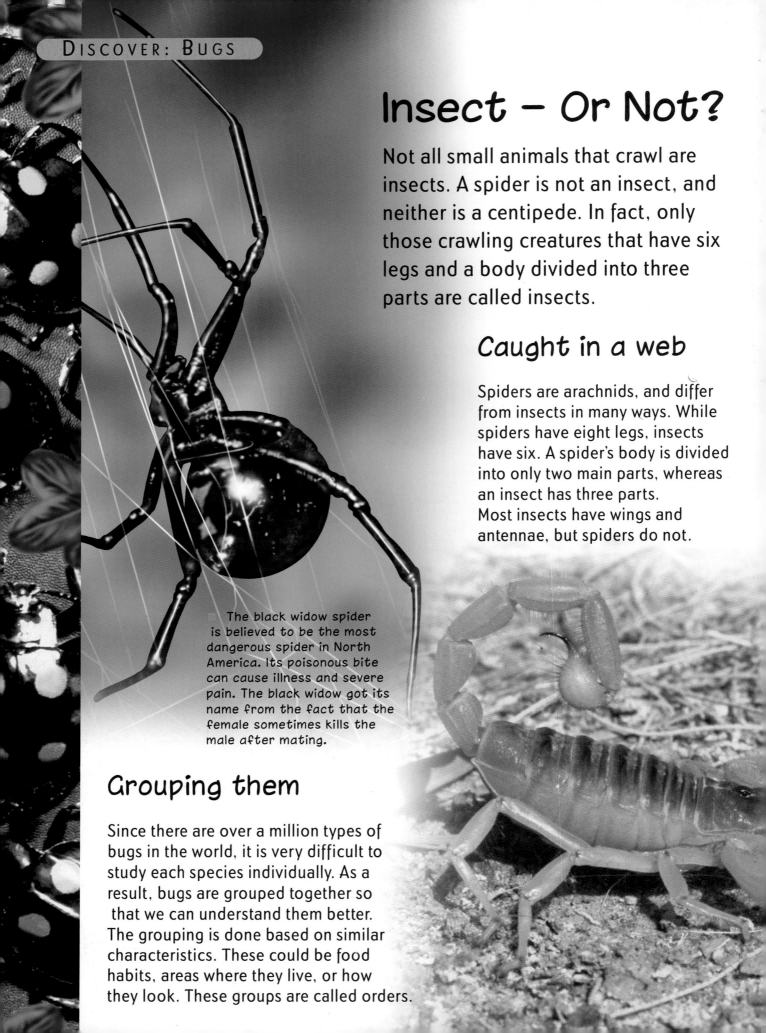

The black widow spider is believed to be the most dangerous spider in North America. Its poisonous bite can cause illness and severe pain. The black widow got its name from the fact that the female sometimes kills the male after mating.

Grouping them

Since there are over a million types of bugs in the world, it is very difficult to study each species individually. As a result, bugs are grouped together so that we can understand them better. The grouping is done based on similar characteristics. These could be food habits, areas where they live, or how they look. These groups are called orders.

FACT FILE

Life spans

Tarantula
Can live up to 30 years
Queen termite
Known to live up to 50 years
Locust
Up to 17 years
Wood beetle
40 years
Mayfly
Just a few hours or one day

■ Although both centipedes and millipedes look similar, they are very different. Centipedes, like this giant desert centipede, can grow up to 8 inches (20 cm) in length, while millipedes are not longer than 4 inches (10 cm). Most centipedes are venomous, while millipedes roll into a ball when threatened.

INTERESTING FACT!

Centipedes and millipedes are not insects. They have narrow bodies divided into segments. Centipedes have one pair of legs per segment, and can have 15 to 175 pairs of legs. Millipedes have 2 pairs of legs per segment, with up to 350 pairs of legs!

Some disagreement

Entomologists, or people who study bugs, do not agree on the number of orders that exist. Some may consider a certain group of bugs as a single order, but others might regard them as two or more orders. For this reason, some say that there are more than 30 orders, and others list fewer than 25.

■ Scorpions are also arachnids, not insects. They have a poisonous sting at the end of their tails. In some species this sting is capable of killing a human.

Naming game

The orders are arranged according to how bugs have developed over millions of years. Since most orders are based on similar features, the name of the order tells us about a particular feature. The feature is usually given at the end of the name as a suffix. The suffix -ura means tail, -ptera means wings, and -aptera means wingless.

Bug Senses

Insects depend on their senses of touch, hearing, smell, sight and taste to find their way home, locate food, and protect themselves. While bugs have several special sense organs, the most crucial are the antennae. The sensory deprivation caused by removing an insect's antennae renders individuals of many species helpless.

■ Some kinds of bugs – including ants, bees and wasps – have taste organs on their antennae. They touch the food with their antennae, and eat it only if they like the taste. Other bugs – including flies, honeybees, butterflies, and some moths – taste with their feet!

Many lenses

Most bugs have two large compound eyes on their head. While humans have just one lens in each eye that enables them to focus on objects, bugs have many lenses. Each eye is made up of tiny, six-sided lenses that fit together like a honeycomb.

Smelly factor

A bug's antennae also help it to smell things. It uses its sense of smell to look for food, find its way around, and locate places to lay eggs. Ants and bees recognize other members of their colony by their odor.

■ Bugs like the dragonfly can only see a short distance. Objects more than three feet away appear as a blur to them, but they can see broad movements, as well as recognize colors. Bugs have no eyelids, so their eyes are always open.

Touchy creatures

Bugs have excellent sensory perception. They sense the air around them with the hairs and spines that cover their body and antennae. Bugs can even feel a change in the air around them. That is why no matter how carefully you move your hand toward a fly, it will always fly away!

■ Bristles, or fine hairs, on the antennae and the legs help bugs to hear, smell, taste and even feel objects!

■ A bug's ears can be located almost anywhere on the body. For instance, the narrow-beaked katydid has ears on its legs!

INTERESTING FACT!

Bugs do not have actual voices. Many of them rub body parts against each other to make sounds. Crickets rub their legs together to make chirping sounds, while bees make a humming noise by flapping their wings rapidly.

Hear a whisper

Most bugs can hear sounds that are either too soft or too high-pitched for humans. But only a few types of bugs have actual ears. Others hear with the delicate hairs on their antennae and body.

Attack and Defense

A bug's life is filled with dangers. It may be eaten by other bugs, birds or animals. Cold weather may kill it, or a dry spell may kill the plants it eats. People are also a threat. Hence, to fight for survival, bugs have developed special means of defense.

Scooting away

Bugs have many defense mechanisms. The most common is to escape by quickly flying, leaping, or scampering away. Some caterpillars and beetles play dead, or use threatening postures to frighten the enemy. They also use special poses to attack and kill other bugs.

■ The mantis - also called the 'praying mantis' - holds its front legs as if it were praying. It uses its arm-like forelegs to grasp and capture its prey. The mantis is often missed by its prey as well as by its predators, because of its excellent camouflage.

■ Male stag beetles have oddly enlarged jaws. They resemble the horns of a male deer and can be as long as the body of the insect. Male stag beetles use these horns against each other in battles for mating rights.

Weapons of war

Most bugs have weapons with which to deter enemies. Bees, wasps and some ants have poisonous stings. Certain ants, horseflies and other bugs can pinch with their powerful jaws. Some caterpillars have hollow body hairs filled with poison, which break at the slightest touch, releasing the poison. Stinkbugs, lacewings and carrion beetles give off foul odors. Some butterflies, moths and other bugs are also protected simply because they taste bad to their predators!

■ Many spider species eat other spiders. Most female spiders are larger and stronger than male spiders, and occasionally eat the males.

Mimics for life

Some bugs are great mimics – that is, they resemble other bugs. This often protects weaker bugs, if they look like stronger bugs. For example, since a viceroy butterfly resembles the monarch butterfly, birds leave it alone, because the monarch tastes unpleasant to them.

Coloring camouflage

Some bugs also escape their enemies because either their color or form blends with the surroundings. This is called camouflaging. When resting on tree trunks, many moths look like bark or bird droppings. Stick bugs and some caterpillars resemble twigs.

■ Some butterflies are experts at camouflaging. When a leaf butterfly folds its wings, it looks like a dead leaf.

Bees and Wasps

Some groups of bugs stay in huge colonies. They are called social insects. Termites, ants, bees and wasps are all social insects. These colonies are highly organized.

All in a family

Social insects live in communities where each member depends upon the others. Those living together are part of the same family. For example, the 60,000 to 80,000 bees in a hive are all born from one queen. So are the millions of termites that may make up a termite colony.

■ A hornet is a kind of wasp that lives in large nests that are shaped like an upside-down pear. These usually hang from branches or leaves.

■ Most social wasps make nests of "paper." The female produces the paper by chewing up plant fibers or old wood. The paper is spread in thin layers to make cells where eggs are laid.

Shared work

Each member of a colony does different work, based on its role. The queen's job is to lay eggs. The adults in the colony, called workers, feed and care for the young. Termites have both male and female workers, though all the workers among ants, bees and wasps are females.

FACT FILE

For one pound of honey, bees fly over 55,000 miles (88,514 km)

An average worker bee makes 1/12 of a teaspoon of honey in her lifetime

Honeybees fly at about 15 mph (24 km/h)

An ant can carry 50 times its own weight

Male zone

In many colonies of social insects, males are present for only limited periods of time. Often, the males' only job is to mate with the queen, after which they die. In bee colonies, the males are called drones.

■ Bees eat only nectar. Wasps can feed on other bugs and human food as well.

INTERESTING FACT!

Social insects communicate with one another with the use of sound, touch and scent. Honeybees use a form of dance to tell other members of the hive the direction and distance to where food can be found.

Different tasks

Each colony member performs a specialized task. Nurses look after the young and soldiers defend the colony from attacks by enemies. Some workers search for food, while others enlarge and clean the nest.

■ Cuckoo bees invade the nests of bumblebees and lay eggs there. The bumblebees raise the cuckoos' young as their own.

Ants and Termites

Ants are among the most successful social bugs. While they may look small and simple, they actually have complex behavioral patterns. The division of work in these colonies — including how they get food — is a highly regimented operation.

Special mounds

Termites construct extremely large and elaborate mounds to house their colonies. These mounds take various forms and can be as hard as concrete. On the inside, mounds may have chimneys, a nursery, waste-disposal chambers and a special cell for the queen.

■ The inside of a termite mound is divided into many chambers and galleries. In the center is a closed cell, where the queen lives.

■ The soldier termites (above left) are wingless and blind. They are larger than the workers, with a huge head, powerful jaws and strong legs, but they are not as large as the queen (above right).

Up in arms

Army ants march across huge distances on land and eat other bugs. A single parade of army ants looks so formidable that even bigger creatures are intimidated. Due to their sheer number, army ants can also attack mice and lizards. If the prey is unable to escape quickly, the ants can overwhelm it by swarming all over it.

■ Leafcutter ants continually collect leaves, which they cut into tiny pieces for easier carrying.

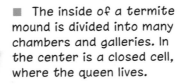

FACT FILE

Termite mounds can be as high as 20 feet (6 m)
Largest ant
over 1 inch (2.5 cm) long
Smallest ant
about 0.04 inch (0.1 cm) long
Queen ant
lives 10-20 years; workers, 1-5 years; while male ants survive for just a few months

Slave drivers

Certain kinds of ants keep aphids, caterpillars, or other bugs which they "milk" for food. Many ants raid other ants' nests and carry off the young, which they bring up as slaves.

■ Weaver ants build nests in trees by attaching leaves together. Bridges of workers first pull in the leaves. These leaves are then sewed up by pressing silk-producing larvae against them.

INTERESTING FACT!

Ants "talk" to one another by giving off chemicals called pheromones. An ant may lay a scent trail from a newly discovered food supply to its nest. The other workers then follow the trail to the food.

Gardeners and thieves

Ants have different ways of gathering food. Harvester ants collect seeds, which are stored in their nests. Thief ants live by stealing food from other ants. Some other species, such as leafcutter ants, actually grow their own food. They cultivate tiny mushroom gardens in their nests!

Winged Wonders

Butterflies are among the most elegant and beautiful insects. They have delicate and often very colorful wings. Butterflies and moths belong to the same order of winged bugs. They are the only bugs to have scales on their wings.

■ Most butterflies rest with their wings held upright over their bodies. Moths, however, rest with their wings spread out flat.

Moth or butterfly?

Although grouped together, moths are not quite the same as butterflies. Moths have plump, furry bodies, while butterflies are slender. Moths also do not have knobs on their antennae like butterflies do. And while butterflies fly during the day, moths prefer nights.

Before take-off

Butterflies and moths cannot fly if their body temperature is too low. They need to warm up first. The bugs either bask in the sun or shake their wings to build up heat.

■ Butterflies attract each other with the colorful patterns on their wings. After mating, the female begins laying eggs within a few hours, but the male dies.

Hungry caterpillar

Butterflies and moths undergo a complete change while going through four different life stages. They start life as an egg. The larva or caterpillar hatches from the egg and feeds on leaves or flowers. As it grows, the caterpillar loses its outer skin – in other words, it molts many times.

■ The Heliconid butterfly is also known as the "passion flower" butterfly. It feeds on the poisonous leaves of the passion flower. This makes it inedible for other animals.

Resting stage

After reaching its full size, the caterpillar turns into a pupa. The pupa is motionless, which is why this is often called the "resting" stage. The adult butterfly is slowly formed within the cocoon. This stage can last from a few days to over a year.

■ Satyrid butterflies, also called wood nymphs, fly at low heights and in a zigzag manner. On sensing danger, the butterflies stay motionless with closed wings. If the danger continues, they fly away.

INTERESTING FACT!

In addition to color and shape, the fragrance of flowers is what really draws butterflies to a garden. Flowers with the strongest perfume are most appealing to a butterfly's sensitive sense of smell.

Along Came a Spider

One of the most common crawling creatures on earth is the spider. But remember that spiders are not insects. They belong to another class called arachnids. Scorpions also belong to that class.

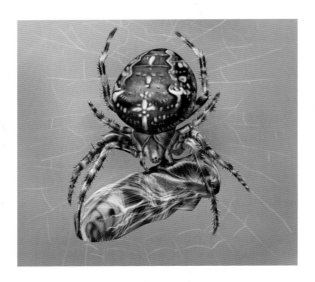

Living zones

Like insects, spiders can live just about anywhere. Spiders are found in fields, woods, swamps, caves and deserts. Spiders help people by eating harmful bugs. They eat grasshoppers and locusts, which destroy crops, and flies and mosquitoes, which carry diseases.

■ A spider never gets caught in its own web. The spider walks across the web, holding on to the silk lines with a special hooked claw on each foot.

■ Most spiders enclose their eggs in a sac. The egg sac is a bag made of a special kind of silk. Some spiders hang their sac in a web. Others attach it to leaves or plants. Still others carry it with them. Spiderlings hatch inside the egg sac.

Spot the difference

The difference between insects and spiders can be seen from their body structure. Spiders have four pairs of legs and only two body segments - a fused head and thorax, and an abdomen.

FACT FILE
Types
more than 30,000
Largest
South American tarantula,
9.8 inches (25 cm) long
Smallest
an orbweb from Samoa
0.02 inches (0.43 mm) long,
about the size of a pinhead
Average egg yield
100; can go up to 2,000

Spinning magic

Spiders produce silk for their web through special glands. The web is spun through short, finger-like organs called spinnerets, which are attached to the abdomen. A spider can have two, four, or six spinnerets. The tip of a spinneret is covered with tubes, through which liquid silk flows from the glands. The silk later hardens into a thread.

Web of death

Spiders love to feed on bugs and spin webs to catch them. Even bugs that are larger and stronger than spiders cannot escape from the threads of a spider's web.

■ Hunting spiders have good eyesight at short distances. Web-building spiders, on the other hand, have poor eyesight. Their eyes are used for detecting changes in light.

INTERESTING FACT!

More than 150 spiders were used in the movie "Spider-Man." They were specially picked for the role. Those who made it to the big screen had the best spider behavior!

■ Orb weavers spin the most beautiful webs. Many orb weavers spin a new web every night. And it takes them just about an hour. These weavers often wrap their victims in "sheets," just like mummies.

Knights in Shining Armor

Beetles are the toughest looking bugs around. Unlike other insects, adult beetles have a pair of special front wings called elytra. They form a leathery cover, protecting the beetle's body. Beetles are called the "armored tanks" of the insect world, because of their hard wings and shell-like exoskeleton.

Amazing variety

Beetles live everywhere on Earth except in the oceans. They vary greatly in shape, color and size. Some, such as click beetles and fireflies, are long and slender. Others, including ladybugs, are round. Most beetles are brown, black or dark red in color, though some can have bright, shiny rainbow colors.

■ Fungus beetles feed on spores of fungi. They also mess up the areas they live in with their waste and cast-off skins.

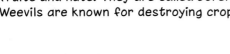
■ The mouths of adult weevils are at the tip of a long snout, which is used to bore into fruits, seeds and other plant parts. The larvae have no legs and feed on the inside of fruits and nuts. They are called borers. Weevils are known for destroying crops.

Legs for work

Like their shape and color, the legs of a beetle also vary. Each of the six legs usually has claws at the end. Fast-running beetles have long, slender legs. Others have short and stout legs, with flat pads that help them walk on slippery surfaces. Digging beetles have tooth-like projections on their legs to scrape away soil. Most swimming beetles have flat hind legs.

INTERESTING FACT!
Click beetles make a clicking sound if disturbed. These beetles have a hook-like part that locks the first and second segments of the thorax. When they release the hook, a sudden body jerk produces a clicking sound.

FACT FILE

Smallest: Feather-winged beetles, less than 0.02 inches (0.5 mm) long.
Largest: the Goliath beetle of Africa grows to about 5 inches (13 cm)
Strongest: American burying beetles can lift 200 times their own weight
Hottest: Bombardier beetles can shoot a hot, smelly liquid 212 °F (100 °C) in temperature from their abdomen

■ Scarab beetles such as dung beetles and tumblebugs feed on dung. They roll the dung into balls and bury it in soil. Females lay one egg in the ball of dung. Some scarabs, like June beetles and Japanese beetles, eat crops.

Mixed bag

Many beetles feed on crops, trees or stored food, causing a lot of damage. Such bugs are called pests. However, some beetles are helpful to people. For example, ladybugs and certain other beetles save crops by eating bugs such as aphids. Other beetles, like the dung beetle, are important because they eat dead plants and animals, clearing the environment.

■ Darkling beetles feed on plants and like to walk around. But when disturbed, they assume a head-down and tail-up position. If handled roughly, they release a dark-colored, foul-smelling fluid. This behavior is enough to ward off most predators.

Enemy protection

Beetles have many enemies, including birds, reptiles and other bugs. Most beetles protect themselves by biting, hiding or flying away. Some beetles produce a bad smell that predators avoid.

Ballet Dancers

Most people would agree that butterflies, dragonflies, and mayflies are very beautiful insects. They have four lacy wings and a slim, long tail that trails behind them. The wings shimmer and gleam in the sunlight when these insects fly. These bugs look so graceful while flying that they are sometimes referred to as the 'ballet dancers' of the bug world!

Nymph's tale

Young mayflies are called nymphs or naiads. Mayflies lay their eggs in streams and ponds. The nymphs breathe through gills, feed on water plants and live for a few months to two years. They shed their skin when they leave the water and become winged subimagos, or subadults. Mayflies are the only bugs to go through this stage. After just hours, the subimago becomes a full-grown adult.

■ Mayflies are commonly called dayflies because of their short lives. Adult mayflies live for only a few hours or a few days.

■ The dragonfly can hover in mid-air by flapping its wings. It eats other bugs, catching them while flying.

Keen eyes

Dragonflies have very good eyesight due to their eye structure. Dragonflies have up to 30,000 facets to their compound eyes. Each one is a separate light-sensing organ, or ommatidium, arranged to give a nearly 360 degree field of vision.

Masking lip

Dragonfly nymphs remain in the water for one to five years. They have a thick body and a big head and mouth, but no wings. They have a folding lower lip, called a mask, which is half as long as their bodies. The lip has jaw-like hooks at the end and can move out to capture prey.

■ Dobson flies resemble dragonflies. However, they cannot fly as well as dragonflies. Also, unlike dragonflies, dobson flies can fold their wings over their backs when not in flight.

FACT FILE

Biggest living dragonfly
Megaloprepus coerulatus;
wingspan about 7 inches
(19 cm)
Smallest
Nannophya pygmaea;
0.6 inches (1.5 cm) long,
wingspan about 0.8 inches
(2 cm)
Dragonflies
can fly up to
60 mph (95 km/h)

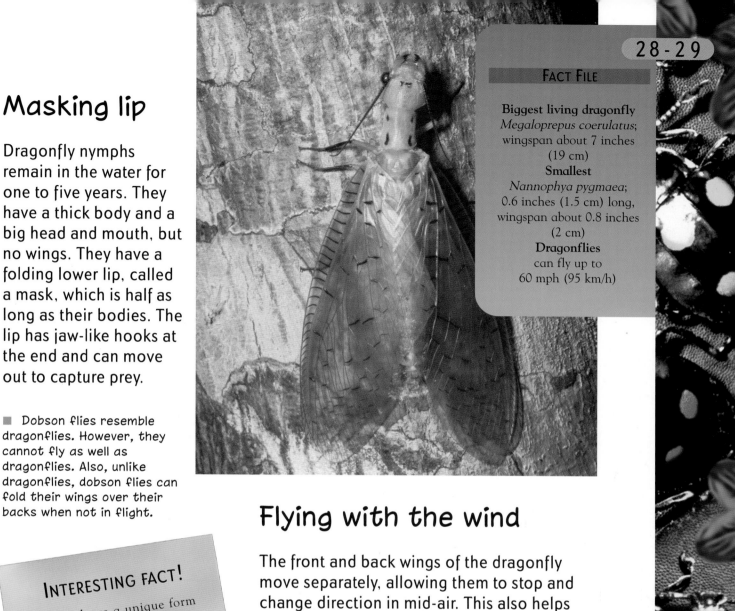

INTERESTING FACT!

Fireflies have a unique form of communication – light! The light organs in a firefly are located on the underside of the abdomen.
A chemical reaction in the light organs produces the firefly's light.

Flying with the wind

The front and back wings of the dragonfly move separately, allowing them to stop and change direction in mid-air. This also helps them to fly at higher speeds. While resting, dragonflies hold their wings open. Their back wings are broader than the front ones.

True Bugs

"True bugs" can be found all over the world. Unlike most other bugs, true bugs have both piercing and sucking mouthparts. These are found in a long, beak-like structure. True bugs mostly feed on plant juices, though some can also suck blood from animals or other bugs.

■ The young of true bugs look like wingless adults. Their metamorphosis does not involve a pupa.

Killers

A variety of insects, including caterpillars and cockroaches, often fall prey to 'assassin' bugs. Assassin bugs lie in wait for other bugs and then stab the prey with their beak. The assassin bug injects a toxin that dissolves the prey's tissue. It then sucks up the other bug. Some assassins can produce hissing sounds by rubbing their feeding tube against the underside of their body.

■ Leaf-footed insects, and especially their young, resemble assassin beetles.

FACT FILE

Number of species
Over 80,000
Length
0.04 inch (1 mm) to
4.3 inches (11 cm)

Half wings

True bugs have a kind of "half" wing, with the front wing divided into a leathery hard part and a membranous softer part. These wing covers are held over the back and are often partly folded.

Pest problems

Many stinkbugs and shield bugs are agricultural pests. They suck plant juices and damage crop production. These bugs are present in large populations. They are also often resistant to the sprays that are used to kill such bugs.

Walking on water

Many true bugs are aquatic. These water striders move on water with their feet barely touching the surface. They detect the ripples of other bugs on the water and run quickly to capture and kill their prey.

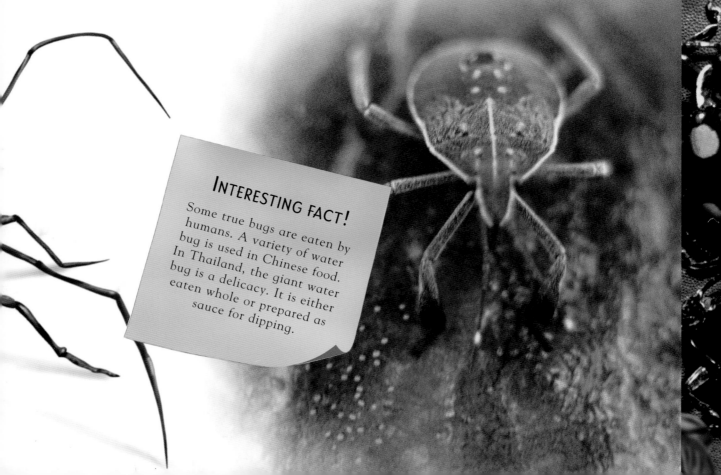

■ Some bugs are capable of producing a foul-smelling chemical with the glands on the sides of their bodies. They are known as stink bugs.

INTERESTING FACT!

Some true bugs are eaten by humans. A variety of water bug is used in Chinese food. In Thailand, the giant water bug is a delicacy. It is either eaten whole or prepared as sauce for dipping.

Camouflage Specialists

Some bugs, like the leaf and stick bugs, are masters of camouflage – that is, they can blend into their surroundings. It is very difficult to spot these bugs in the forest. This special feature helps bugs to hide from enemies. It also allows them to sneak up quietly on their prey.

Blowing in the wind

In order to completely blend into its surroundings, the leaf insect walks by gently swaying its whole body from side to side. It then looks like a leaf blowing in the wind. This perfect camouflage allows the leaf insect to be active during the day.

■ Color plays a major role in camouflage. But it is also important for the insect to remain motionless. The katydid has mastered this art perfectly. A katydid sitting on a leaf can be seen only upon careful examination.

FACT FILE
Leaf insect
Average length 6 inches
(14 cm); can be as long as
10 inches (25 cm)
Stick insect
Average length
4-6 inches (10-15 cm);
can be as long as
20 inches (52 cm)

Hiding in branches

As their names suggest, stick bugs look like branches. You can spot them by looking for a branch that is out of line or attached to the outside edges of leaves. Stick bugs are usually drab in color, but one type of stick bug has a stunning sky-blue color.

Under leaves

Leaf bugs hang from the underside of tree leaves. At first they look like dried, dead leaves and are tough to spot. Their color can range from pale green to dark brown, depending on the color of the leaves.

Protection sprays

Some camouflage bugs also have other defense mechanisms to deter the enemy. The peppermint stick bug sprays an irritating fluid at its predators, the smell of which is similar to a peppermint. The spray can also be foul-smelling.

■ Certain types of stick bugs have projections along the body, which look like the thorns of a plant.

■ Walking stick bugs are long and slow-moving. They feed on plants.

INTERESTING FACT!
Some leaf bugs have broad-ribbed wings that fold over the back in the shape of a leaf. These bugs can also have enlarged, leaf-like growths on the joints of their legs, giving them their particular name.

Garden Party

Domestic gardens are a great place to observe insects. Among the bugs that can be found in a garden are grasshoppers, crickets and cicadas. These garden bugs are either green or brown in color. They feed on plants and the remains of other bugs.

Hopping and walking

Grasshoppers can hop, walk and fly. The long legs at the back are used for hopping, and the bug can leap about 20 times the length of its body. The shorter front legs are used to hold prey as well as to walk.

■ The cicada is a large-bodied, dark-colored flying insect. When at rest, it holds the wings over the body like a tent. Male cicadas are the noisiest insects in the world.

■ Most grasshoppers are bright green, olive green, or brown in color. But rainbow grasshoppers are very colorful.

Eyeing around

A grasshopper has five eyes. Each side of the head has a large compound eye with thousands of single lenses. These eyes allow the bug to see all around. A grasshopper also has three small single eyes. One is above the antennae, one below, and one midway between the two antennae.

FACT FILE

Grasshoppers lay
2 to 120 eggs at a time
They can be as long as
4.5 inches (11 cm)
They can jump to 20 times
their body length
Crickets
can be 0.9 to 3 inches
(2.5 to 7 cm) long

INTERESTING FACT!

Certain species of cicadas, called periodical cicadas, take 13-17 years to develop. Depending upon the species, the nymphs spend about 13-17 years underground before coming out to mate. The adult cicadas die soon after mating!

■ The Jerusalem cricket can be found in moist areas in deserts. Because of its surprisingly human-like head it is called "child of the earth" in some places.

■ Grasshoppers are eaten as a delicacy in many countries. They are a good source of protein. Many countries also instruct their soldiers to eat grasshoppers if they get lost and run out of food.

Song of love

Male crickets are said to "sing" songs. And each kind of cricket has a different song. Some trill, while others make a series of chirps. Crickets produce a musical chirping sound by rubbing their two front wings together. It is this sound that leads female crickets to the male!

Cricket info

Crickets are related to grasshoppers but have many differences. The wings of most crickets lie flat over each other on top of their backs. Other crickets only have tiny wings, or are wingless. The slender antennae are much longer than the body in many of these bugs.

Venom and Stings

A bug bite or a sting can be very painful, and they can be quite dangerous for someone who is allergic. A bug uses its bite or sting for two purposes. The first is for protection from enemies. A bite can scare off an ememy – or even paralyze it. The other use is to get food. Bugs that feed on other bugs use this tactic.

■ Scorpions perform dance-like movements while mating.

Bee sting

Most bees depend on their stingers for defending their homes. The stinger of a worker bee is straight, with hooks on it. When the bee thrusts the stinger into the flesh, the hook holds tight and the stinger pulls out of the bee's body. Glands attached to the stinger produce a poison, which is pumped in.

Death of the worker

Queen bees have a smooth, curved stinger that is used to kill other queens. Queens do not lose their stingers like worker bees. A worker bee dies soon after losing its stinger. Drones have no stinger.

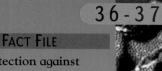

■ The earwig gets its name from the belief that it crawls into the ears of humans and lays eggs in their brains! However, this is not true. Earwigs are harmless to humans. But if carelessly handled, the insect can give you a painful pinch with its pincers!

Spider venom

Almost all spiders have venom, which they inject into their victims to paralyze them. But very few spiders are actually venomous enough to cause injury to humans. Some of the commonly found venomous spiders that are harmful to humans include black widow, brown recluse and yellow sac spiders. Although the venom of a black widow is considered highly toxic, hardly any deaths have ever been reported. The bite can, however, be painful and may cause severe adverse reactions.

Venom kills

Scorpions and centipedes are among the most poisonous creatures on earth. They can kill humans and big animals. Both are often mistaken for insects, although they are not.

INTERESTING FACT!

Killer bees are very dangerous. If their hive is disturbed, they attack anything in the surrounding area. They attack in large numbers and their stings can kill people.

House Creatures

Bugs can feel very much at home in your house! The warm conditions and a multitude of ideal hiding spots, as well as plentiful food supplies, make the average home an attractive domain.

Dinner time

Female mosquitoes drink blood, while males only sip plant nectar. Houseflies cannot bite or chew, but they can liquefy many solid foods with their saliva. Cockroaches, on the other hand, are scavengers. They will eat a variety of substances, including book binding, paper, soap, plants and dead animals.

■ Certain kinds of mosquitoes carry germs that cause diseases like encephalitis, malaria and yellow fever. When a mosquito bites you, it may leave germs behind.

INTERESTING FACT!

The buzzing of a fly is actually the noise of its wings beating. A housefly's wings beat about 200 times a second. A mosquito makes more noise, with its wings moving about 1,000 times a second.

■ Termites live on trees and have a long, nose-like snout. Some can spray glue from their nose, using it to trap other bugs and kill them!

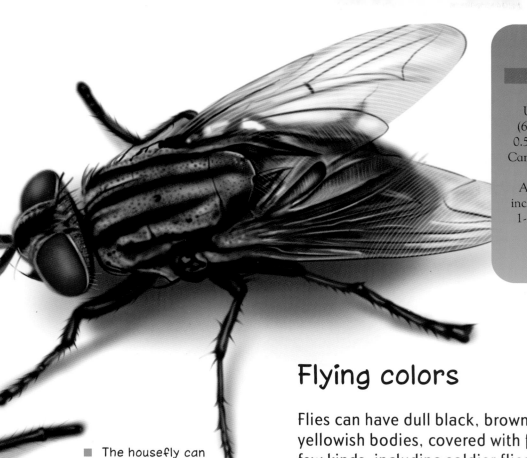

FACT FILE

Housefly
Up to 0.25-0.35 inches
(6-9 mm) long; wingspan
0.5-0.6 inches (13-15 mm)
Can fly at 4.3 mph (7 km/h)
Mosquito
Average length 0.1-0.25
inches (3-6 mm); can fly at
1-1.5 mph (1.6-2.4 km/h)
Cockroach
Can run up to 3 mph
(5 km/h)

■ The housefly can be a carrier of diseases such as typhoid fever, cholera, dysentery and anthrax.

Flying colors

Flies can have dull black, brown, gray, or yellowish bodies, covered with fine hair. A few kinds, including soldier flies and hover flies, may have bright orange, white or yellow markings. Some others, such as bluebottles and greenbottles, are shiny blue or green.

Brown and crawly

Cockroaches have flat, oval bodies. Their long legs are covered with bristles that help them feel things. Cockroaches are fast runners, and many of them can also fly. These bugs have long antennae with organs that can detect certain smells.

■ A cockroach can hold its breath for 40 minutes. If its head is removed, a cockroach can go on living for up to a week.

Keeping them away

The best way to keep bugs away is to keep the house clean. It is best not to keep old newspapers or allow dirty water to stagnate. Any crack in the wall should be sealed, as young cockroaches can crawl into gaps only 0.02 inches (0.5 mm) wide. One can also use sprays or other insect repellents. Mosquitoes and cockroaches are tough survivors, though.

Bugs That Harm

Very few insect species are harmful to humans. Less than one percent of all bugs are really dangerous. But these few can create a lot of havoc. They can eat crops, invade houses, and damage clothes and furniture. They can also infect humans and livestock with diseases.

■ Ticks, like fleas, are tiny, bloodsucking animals that live on other animals and humans. But unlike fleas, ticks are not insects. They are, in fact, related to spiders.

Crop-eaters

Bugs attack almost all types of plants. The major pests include Hessian flies, which attack wheat; boll weevils, which eat up cotton crops; and corn earworms and chinch bugs, which destroy corn and other crops. Colorado beetles feed on potatoes. Bugs like locusts attack in swarms and can eat up an entire crop field in minutes.

Life-threatening

Houseflies and blowflies carry germs and deposit them in our food or water. These germs cause diseases like typhoid fever, cholera and dysentery. Insect bites can also cause deadly illnesses like dengue fever, encephalitis, malaria, African sleeping sickness and bubonic plague. Some bugs like fleas and lice live on human bodies and suck their blood.

Home invaders

Bugs create a mess in homes. Cloth moths and carpet beetles make holes in clothes, sofas and carpets. Silverfish can damage books, while termites will burrow into anything made of wood. Ants and cockroaches spoil food and can also transport germs.

■ Mites are smaller versions of ticks and mostly live on decaying matter. But some live on humans and animals. The young of the red velvet mite live on grasshoppers and locusts, while the adults prey on termites.

INTERESTING FACT!

Predators, parasites, and diseases can all be used to control pests. When the cottony cushion bug posed a threat to California's lemon and orange orchards, ladybugs were brought in to eat up the pests.

Kill them fast!

The easiest way to kill a harmful bug is to swat it the minute you see it! But it is not always safe to do that, especially if there are a large number of bugs present. Another option is to use chemicals called insecticides, which kill the pests. Keep in mind that insecticides can be harmful to the environment.

■ Many beetles have been found to be harmful to crops. The rhinoceros beetle is a common pest in the tropical regions. It bores into the trunks and leaves of coconut trees and feeds on the tender tissues.

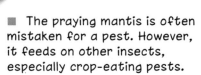

■ The praying mantis is often mistaken for a pest. However, it feeds on other insects, especially crop-eating pests.

Bugs That Help

Some bugs can be very helpful for humans. They help in pollination, make products such as honey, feed on harmful bugs, and serve as food for birds and other animals.

Cleaning agents

Bugs help to keep the landscape clean by feeding on animal wastes and dead animals, and also on the remains of dead plants. Bugs that live in the ground enrich the soil with their waste products and dead bodies.

■ Dung beetles eat dung. They either make a ball out of it, or simply dig burrows under or near the food. This eating habit of the dung beetle not only reduces the piles of manure but also improves the quality of soil and helps to control pests and flies.

Sweet honey

Honeybees suck up nectar from flowers and store it in their honey stomachs. They return to the hive and spit the nectar out into it. The worker bees in the hive then add enzymes to the nectar. As the water in the nectar evaporates, the nectar changes into honey!

■ Honeybees communicate by dancing. The dance tells worker bees where to find nectar.

■ The ladybug
eats several kinds of
crop-destroying bugs.

FACT FILE

Honeybees must tap
some 2 million flowers to
make 1 pound of honey
They fly over
55,000 miles (88,514 km) for
1 pound of honey
Honeybee flies
15 mph (24 km/h); visits 50
to 100 flowers in one trip

INTERESTING FACT!

Some helpful bugs act as
parasites, living in - or on -
the bodies of harmful bugs.
For example, some wasps lay
their eggs in caterpillars that
damage tomato plants. As
the young wasps develop,
they feed on the caterpillars.

■ Silkworm cocoons
are harvested for the
production of silk. The
cocoons are usually
boiled to help unravel
the tightly bonded silk
and the silkworm is
then often eaten as a
delicacy.

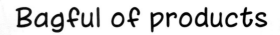

Bagful of products

Bugs provide us with many
valuable products. These include
honey and beeswax, made by bees;
shellac, made from a substance
given off by lac bugs; and silk,
produced by silkworms.

Spinning silk

A silkworm is not a worm, but
the larva of a moth. A silkworm
feeds only on mulberry leaves. It
spins a cocoon from which raw
silk is obtained. The cocoon is
made of a single, continuous
thread of raw silk, which is 1,000
to 3,000 feet (300 to 900m) long.

Glossary

Adaptability: A living organism's ability to change or be changed to suit its surroundings or environment

Anthrax: An infectious disease found among warm-blooded animals, especially cattle and sheep. It is caused by the bacterium *Bacillus anthracis*

Aphid: A small, soft-bodied insect of the family Aphididae. It has mouthparts used for piercing and sucking plant sap

Arachnid: Has four pairs of legs but no antennae, no wings and only two body segments - a fused head and thorax, and an abdomen.

Camouflage: A bug's natural method of concealing itself from an enemy by appearing to be part of its surroundings

Carrion: A dead or decaying animal

Cholera: A disease of the small intestine caused by the bacteria *vibrio cholerae*. Symptoms include vomiting, upset stomach, muscle cramps and dehydration

Dengue: A type of fever found in the tropics. It is caused by mosquitoes and symptoms include rash, headaches, and joint pain

Encephalitis: A disease where the patient suffers inflammation of the brain. Symptoms include headache, drowsiness, nausea and fever

Habitat: An environment where an organism lives and multiplies

Insect: A small animal that has six legs and a body divided into three parts - head, thorax, and abdomen. The head has a pair of antennae and compound eyes

Larva: The wingless, wormlike form of bugs that hatches from an egg

Lens: A transparent tissue that is found behind the iris in the eye

Malaria: An infectious disease carried by the Anopheles mosquito. Symptoms include fever and shivering

Metamorphosis:
The total transformation a larva undergoes into its adult stage

Naiad: A life stage of some aquatic insects

Pheromone: A chemical substance that an organism gives out, as a signal to others of the same species

Pollination: The process by which pollen is transferred to help a plant reproduce

Predator: An animal that preys on other animals for its food

Pupa: The stage of development of an insect between its larva and adult phases

Species: A group of organisms that have identical traits and can interbreed

Spinneret: Special organ situated under the abdomen of spiders, used to spin webs

True Bug: An insect with mouthparts capable of piercing and sucking

Yellow fever: Infectious disease caused by a virus carried by the Aedes mosquito. Symptoms include fever, muscle cramps, headache and backache

Further Reading

Books

Healy, Nick. *The World's Most Dangerous Bugs.* Mankato, MN: Capstone Press, 2006.

Huggins-Cooper, Lynn. *Beastly Bugs.* North Mankato, MN: Smart Apple Media, 2007.

Phillips, Dee. *Bugs and Spiders.* Minnetonka, MN: Two-Can Publishing, 2006.

Smithyman, Kathryn and Bobbie Kalman. *Insects in Danger.* New York: Crabtree Publishing, 2006.

Internet Addresses

Pest World for Kids
http://www.pestworldforkids.org/home.asp

Insects
http://www.ars.usda.gov/is/kids/insects/insectintro.htm

What Is an Insect?
http://kids.yahoo.com/animals/insects

Index